POETRY

now

Poets Bite Back

Edited by

Andrew Head

First published in Great Britain in 1998 by
POETRY NOW
1-2 Wainman Road, Woodston,
Peterborough, PE2 7BU
Telephone (01733) 230746
Fax (01733) 230751

HB ISBN 0 75430 529 5
SB ISBN 0 75430 530 9

FOREWORD

Although we are a nation of poetry writers we are accused of not reading poetry and not buying poetry books: after many years of listening to the incessant gripes of poetry publishers, I can only assume that the books they publish, in general, are books that most people do not want to read.

Poetry should not be obscure, introverted, and as cryptic as a crossword puzzle: it is the poet's duty to reach out and embrace the world.

The world owes the poet nothing and we should not be expected to dig and delve into a rambling discourse searching for some inner meaning.

The reason we write poetry (and almost all of us do) is because we want to communicate: an ideal; an idea; or a specific feeling. Poetry is as essential in communication, as a letter; a radio; a telephone, and the main criteria for selecting the poems in this anthology is very simple: they communicate.

This anthology is as the title states; a poetic grump and gripe of what really gets your back up.

Written by well acclaimed Poetry Now writers, this anthology is sure to get your pulse rate soaring and your poetic ability pulsing.

Topics such as office days and supermarket trolleys have all come under fire and I'm sure you will find this anthology a lingering reminder to all those Monday morning and wrong side of the bed style days.

Contents

WARNING

I'm writing these words with growing concern
It seems there's a lesson we still have to learn
That the land and the sea have all had enough
It doesn't want any more of our poisonous stuff
Rivers and streams and even the sky
Will I'm quite sure clog up and die
I've never known anything who'd put up with so much
Watching us daily destroy with our touch
Trees that give life are systematically torn down
To make way for more grazing or expanding a town
The seas are so toxic they cause unimaginable harm
With chemicals from industry and pesticides from farms
That our children will inherit a great barren rock
Unless we this day turn back the clock
And look at a world in serious trouble
That needs everyone's help right now at the double
It'll take a lot of hard work but we can stop the rot
Let's save Mother Earth she's all that we've got.

Michael Bellerby

PRIORITIES

Today I heard a woman
Talking about her pet rabbit
Explaining why she had paid
Several hundred pounds
On dental treatment, adding
That it was money well spent.

Today a television advert
Had a juicy lump of fish
On a bone china plate
Garnished with a sprig of parsley
Delicately placed on a thick rug
For a pampered cat.

Today a bloated bag
Of hanging flesh and wasted bones
Sits in the dirt and dust
Human, hungry and homeless:
Only the buzz of flies
Disturbs the silence.

Richard Stewart

Mindless Actions

Wearing trainers you do not hear their approach, only the shouts
Of exuberant noise fuelled by drugs, drink or sniffing glue.
Damage to car paintwork or aerials will result - no doubt
Or the telephone boxes smashed again by these mindless few.

The sound of splintering panels echo in the still night air
Four youths' running feet pound the road as one, racing out of sight.
The start of wanton damage will now be continued elsewhere
As cleaning crews in the area discover at first light.

Just passing through on the way home bored by the disco or club
Does this destruction make them feel proud, remorseful or ask why?
Will discussing the next target take place mid-week in the pub
Or a change of heart before caught and relatives horrify?

Two telephone boxes stand opposite still in daily use
State of the art mechanism defeated the cash-box thief.
The broken panes removed but not replaced has solved the abuse
Nature's inclement weather offers the public no relief.

Mary E Beale

FALSE FRIENDS

Simply . . . openly, concealing the 'root' of guile.
Exposed 'to show' obvious traits.
Difficult to reconcile
With hidden concentrates . . .
With *that* . . . set out meanwhile . . .
To illustrate
Their style.

Too late, we poor, honest fools see the puerile,
Utterly childish, boastful inmate
Decked out to woo, beguile . . .
See how they, with words, inflate . . .
Set out, compose, compile . . .
A non-existent state . . .
A facsimile . . .

We are taken in by the charade, juvenile . . .
Acted 'part' . . . one they do create . . .
No truth in word, or smile.
Such friends we learn to hate . . .
Then retreat and revile.
To seek to escape . . .
                    is futile.

Brenda J Robson Eifler

Bite Back

How dare that guy on the bus say how bad it was years ago
I do not know where he came from but my friends and I had
loving parents I do know
They worked cooked queued, always there
Had happy surprises - full of cheer

Parents did it for us, they carried the load
In London through the war
I really do not know how they did it, could not have done anymore

They had the first war, then the second
They were our backbone
Did not get handouts, now it would not be known

They put the country first - polite, good manners
They all deserved medals

No doubt there were opportunists
But not that you would notice
What you did notice were people outside little bombed-out
houses at the back of the Stationery Office
trying to rescue belongings

We never knew what we would see when we came out of the shelter
Old Alf the postman walked until he found bombed-out
people - a great helper

I made lots of friends in America
But so sorry I left without saying 'So long' to many
people in England
You would be hard-pressed to find people, such as they were
in those days in this land, especially in London
In England.

Phyllis O'Connell

MACHO MAN

Drive too close, drive too fast, drive too aggressive,
Macho man.

Fill up space, fill up gaps, fill up time,
Macho man.

Pick up skirt, pick up babes, pick up weights,
Macho man.

Cut them up, cut them out, cut them off,
Macho man.

Beat the lights, beat the wife, beat the weak,
Macho man.

Screw the tax, screw the chicks, screw the rivals,
Macho man.

Bump the queue, bump the car, bump and barge,
Macho man.

Play the field, play the game, play the hard man,
Macho man.

Hate the soft, hate the needs, hate the female,
Macho man.

Outside lane, outside right, outside feeling,
Macho man.

Win that bread, win that fight, win a life?
Macho man.

Janet R Holland

VOTE FOR ME

Vote for me the billboard screams
Vote for me, trip of your dreams
Vote for me on 'pick of the week'
Vote for me or the future's bleak
Vote for me the banner said
Vote for me, vote blue, vote red
  Vote for me says the beauty queen
  Vote for me on the silver screen
  Vote for me says the product hype
  Vote for me says the headline type
  Vote for me says the latest brand
  Vote for me, take the world in hand
  Vote for me says the chat show host
  Father, son and holy ghost
  Vote for me says the company chair
  Vote for a merger, vote for a pair
    I'm tired of the listening, tired of the push
    Tired of the pressure, tired of the rush
    Fed-up with choosing, picking a brand
    Saving the world and taking in hand
    All of the things that I'm meant to do
    To live in this world alongside of you
    Alongside the TV, alongside the hype,
    Alongside the chat shows, alongside the type

It's all just for profit, you don't care about me
It's just economics, nothing for 'we'
So go take your products, and go take your phone
Go take your mail and leave me
alone.

Angela Alderton

Leg Room

In trains, planes or theatres or any restricted place
men who sit with their legs open wide with their knees invading my
space
are heading for trouble - more than their delicate ego is going
to be shattered
It's not going to be only fish or wives who end up being battered
There must be a better dictum than 'a woman's place is in the home'
I don't expect men (or women) to sit like they're made of stone
but I know I'm going to allow the heel of my shoe to catch their ankle
not that I want to permanently cripple but their presumption really
does rankle
They think 'no one is going to mind' and they don't have the grace
to apologise - they look at you with surprise on their face
if you voice a protest, their look says 'Oh but I'm a man' (From Mars?)
and then become more histrionic than any of Hollywood's stars.

In trains, planes or theatres or anywhere that seats are close together
men's knees invade others' space and all you get is blether
about the difference in male and female - we all know the form
but if they try to invade my space and explain 'it is the norm'
I'll just explode one of these days and really start ranting and raving
so beware, control your legs or more than your face will need saving
What is it that makes men think that it's their inalienable right
to stretch out and spread themselves when women are squashed up tight
We've achieved discarding tight corsets so let us inhale a deep breath
and declare 'If anyone invades my space he'll achieve a sudden death!'

F Broomfield

My Perfect World

Can you tell me why it is
The more I want
The less there is
Or if I want
To give something away
Then I can't find it
Well at least not today
And many times I think to myself
Right, now, I'll go and put up that shelf
Get it all out and put it half up
Then I just leave it 'cos I've had enough
If I cut the lawn
I leave bits sticking up
Unlocking a door
My key gets stuck
Smoke like a chimney
Drink like a fish
God, bet my mouth's lovely to kiss!
But I'm still here and here I'll stay
At least until my dying day
Then I'll be gone to God knows where
And do you know
I don't care!

Yahoo

The Rats Look Out For Themselves

(With apologies to furry creatures)

The rats are leaving a sinking ship:
Make way! Make way! Make way!
For panic's holding them in its grip:
Touché! Touché! Touché!

With grim foreboding they have foreseen
Disaster threatens all.
Self-preservation's a fine routine -
Save Number One's the call.

The anxious snouts and the honeyed teeth
Make their direction plain.
There may be someone caught underneath,
But others get the gain.

'Oh, are we trampling on rats like us?
A pity there's no time.
But if they're dead, they won't make a fuss.
Survival is no crime.'

The ship was handsome, and in its day
With honour sailed the seas.
A shell now, all that it can display
Are rats that show DTs.

But all will die, for the ship's not sound:
They can't get out in time;
The ocean waves will their greed confound
In grotesque pantomime.

The wavelets bubble above the ship,
The squeaking's heard no more.
Rat ghosts forever will spar and nip
Upon the ocean floor.

Anne Sanderson

TOBACCO ROW

It litters the streets with dirty yellow stubs;
It coats the open road with a special kind of tar;
It fouls the air with its filthy little clouds;
It breaks out into blisters and pustules of puff;
It fuels debates on pollution and contamination;
It gives governments and town councils a splitting headache;
It befuddles board meetings with its ashtray haze;
It exploits the world's poor to profit the stinking rich;
It provides fat-cat tobacco companies with oodles of wealth;
It gave Nosmo King his showbiz name;
It infects shopping centres, invades local amenities;
It divides public transport into special compartments;
It segregates communities, partitions public buildings;
It forms smoke pockets in clean-air zones;
It flares up into family disputes, communal quarrels;
It leads to blazing rows between doctors and patients;
It sets fire to clothes and burns down houses;
It destroys whole forests, devours cities and towns;
It wreaks havoc on the London Underground;
It creates a fog that stings your eyes and makes them smart;
It fills your nose with noisome odours, acrid fumes;
It gives you bad breath and a croaky voice;
It sticks in your throat and clogs your gullet;
It suffocates you, chokes you, robs you of breath;
It lines your lungs with layers of nicotine;
It brings on bronchitis and bronchial pneumonia;
It produces asthma, lung cancer and heart disease;
It causes cot deaths and poisons unborn babies;
It kills people in their thousands every year.

Why don't we just stop growing it altogether?

Robert D Hayward

SHOP TILL YOU DROP

What angers me most
Is ignorance and greed,
The urge to go shopping
For things we don't need.

To be covered in labels
And dripping in gold,
These become our armour
To make us feel bold.

We climb social ladders
To escape from our past,
Chasing a dream
That neither exists nor will last

The need to be someone
Other than ourselves
Using media-based values
We've bought off the shelves.

Perhaps we'll feel better
If we buy some new clothes
So we charge down the motorway
Arriving in droves.

It's off to the shops
To recreate our dream
Leaving us empty, dissatisfied,
Hollow and mean.

Louise Jutton

Gone Nine - We're Late Again

There's a vein pulsing deep in my head,
My teeth are clenched shut at the jaw,
I'm standing with one angry foot,
Positioning open the door.

I've screamed till my voice is quite hoarse,
I'll admit that I'm losing my cool
And all because yet again
They're not ready for school.

I've listened to all the excuses,
I've tried the old 'counting to ten',
But it fell on deaf ears
And I'm nearly in tears,
'They won't play out ever again'!

As if to make matters worse,
When we finally get to the door,
One remembers an obscure thing
She absolutely must bring,
That's never been mentioned before.

So, upstairs and downstairs we go,
Shouting abuse all the way,
And it's not much comfort to know
Tomorrow's another day.

It's not over once that we're off,
'Cause she's left her spellings behind,
Which I know if we should return
Would take an hour to find.

Still, we finally jump from the car,
Now I'm wearing my saintly smile,
And *everybody* smiles back . . .
Clenching their teeth all the while.

Anne Pratt

Supposed To Be Progress

Gone are the days of the human touch,
when a human being could do so much.
Simple things like the telephone
I'm sorry but it makes me moan.
I ring a number and what do I get,
Press star button, choose from a set.
Press one, two or three, it's my choice,
advised by this monochromatic voice.
But I only have a query
by this time I'm more than weary.
Gone is the operator with the happy tone,
in the name of progress and the telephone.
Why with progress has it all gone to pot,
supposed to be better! I think not.
Give me back the service we once knew,
when a polite operator put me through,
Or answered queries quite polite,
was there for us both day and night.
Before progress people seemed to care,
and I for one had much more hair.
Turn back progress, it's a sin,
that's the reason my hair is thin.
You see it makes me scream and shout,
and then I go and pull it out.
Give us back the service we used to know,
give so-called progress the big 'heave-ho'!

Irene Keeling

Simple Choice

The world is made up
Of givers and takers
There are those who are honest
And those who are ruthless
There's good and there's bad
The strong and the weak
It's a question of choices
So to speak

There are happy souls and miserable
There are meek or bold
There are some that don't mind
Some that dread growing old
And that is the way we all get along
By wailing a dirge
Or singing a song

Next time when the devil's
Perched up on your shoulder
Just brush him away, tell him
Push off and move over . . . then
With a spring in your step
Instead of a sting in your tail
The world will be brighter
Your life happier as well.

The message is simple
Maybe, you think somewhat naive
But it works, just you try it
My choice . . . is not to deceive.

Sheila Margaret Parker

'Phone Phobia

As I lie soaking in the bath, the 'phone rings.
In the aftermath, I reach for towel then slip on soap.
It's that long-awaited call I hope
But when I rush half-dried into the hall,
An eerie silence reigns over all.
The 'phone has ceased its strident din.
Can you believe the state I'm in?
Even from 1471 my fickle caller has withdrawn.

Dear Alexander Graham Bell,
You have condemned my soul to hell!
That constant ringing in my ears
Reduces me to helpless tears.

I hire a video for the night,
A Top Ten film for my delight
But, as the tension rises high,
That intrusive predator just makes me sigh.
Why do my friends all wish to 'phone
When all I want is to be left alone?

In comfy bed I stretch out warm
And, drifting off to sleep, I yawn.
I bid a hectic day goodbye.
In slumber sweet I yearn to lie.
Then, from the darkness, a piercing ring.
A wrong number now for my great sin.

Dear Alexander Graham Bell,
You have condemned my soul to hell!
That constant ringing in my ears
Reduces me to helpless tears.

Rosemary Thomson

Why?

Lots of things annoy, and there comes a time when
In my head I scream 'Please don't do that again.'

Why do people put back in the box a blackened used match?
Or when bitten by an insect why do they continue to scratch?

Although we are all human - everyone does annoying things
Like not rinsing out the bath and leaving dirty rings!

When going on my holiday - off to sunny Spain
Then suddenly I'm delayed; of course it is the plane.

Things like this do happen, these times I do hate
When someone says 7.00 o'clock, why are they late?

Another frequent happening - some people have a flair
To rudely wait and stand and continually stare!

I'm waiting for a parcel, promised today without a doubt
Why on nipping to the shop, does the postman call when I am out?

I have an answerphone for a reason, in case I'm not at home
Why listen to the message and then put down the phone?

Then of course the salesman - I'm sure you're not amazed
While knocking on my door can't they see I'm double-glazed?

And why does my partner after making a cup of tea
Put the empty milk carton in the fridge for all of us to see?

Or when he weeds the garden, I've noticed for a while
Why does he leaves the weeds on the lawn in a pile?

I've said my thoughts now - I'm going while I'm able
Before he comes home - I must tidy this kitchen table!

Michelle Peacock

Grave Mistakes

I *cannot understand*
People who walk and talk with cigarettes
in their hand.
There's a place
For the weed, it's called an ashtray,
Not my face!
They saturate my lucidity with their insensitivity
And frustrate
My breathing -
Cause annoyance and asthma attacks,
Leaving me seething
With indignation,
Not being able to escape second-hand smoke
Inhalation.
Total dissatisfaction
Created by uncaring pollutists, blissfully unaware
of reprobation.
Grave mistakes
Walk and talk hand in hand with he
who partakes.

Patricia McDonald

Selective Xenophobia

Those blasted *****s,
Why can't they use the dump
like responsible suburbanites?
Ditching glass and guttering,
and glass and shattered boughs,
and glass and airgun-peppered cans,
and breaking glass (I loathe the sound!).

They don't care a *****,
They run a spotless, white BMW out front
And dump detritus at the back - *our* back!

What do they think of us?
Not much it seems.
I know what neighbours think of them,
Why don't they shove off back to ***** or *****
and pollute their own backyard?

These thoughts of malice seethe as -
with double garden glove-protected hands -
I pick up, *dig* up, five boxes'worth
of spiteful, glinting shards,
load them in grubby, white Sierra
and run them to the dump.

But . . . those other *****s aren't bad.
In fact, they're rather nice.
He helped me with my car once.
You couldn't meet a more obliging chap,
Well, alright, *they* can stay -
but the rest can shove off, blasted *****s.

Hold on, though . . . what starts with 'blasted *****s'
can end in genocide!

What if they weren't *****s?
Well . . . they'd just be . . . blighters.

Wes Ashwell

Train Mayhem

When will it come they start to shout,
It won't be long I have no doubt,
While lips that smile start to pout,
As minutes soon add up to hours,
When the smiles gradually sours,
Then the trains start to run,
When will our horrid train come?

British Rail 'are getting there',
Without knowing precisely where,
As usual it is getting late,
No matter to where or what the date,
This time it's only a three-hour wait.
'Getting there'! we begin to smile
As away the hours we sit and wile.

Is this the one? I'm getting cold and wet.
If we had gambled, we would lose the bet.
As the children start to weep,
At least the baby has gone to sleep.
'Is that our train?' the children cry.
'I wish it was' my wistful sigh
As I begin to wonder why!

Children put their fingers in their ears,
As through your brain that awful sound sears,
Of all the trains going in and out
While above the noise they try to shout,
'Mind the doors,' stand back I pray
As the train begins to sway,
'At last!' you will hear me say.

Out of the station homeward bound,
An end to all that dreadful sound,
That makes my old head pound.
Onward to our journey's end,
Rushing to our home and friends.
Saying to all '*Never ever again*
Will we travel on the train!'

Janet Allwright

Bite Back

I hate many things
Happening here on Earth,
Especially some efforts
Which tend to make life worse.

I hate seeing the starving,
The dying here on Earth,
When all could be so perfect,
And no one need be hurt.

I hate seeing the crippled,
From war and crazy ways,
The maimed from wars still struggling,
To live a life again.

I hate pornography
And writings that procure,
A wickedness on Earth,
When we need mind cures.

I hate tuneless music,
For harmony refines,
The mind to brainly functions
And healing music binds.

I hate all cruelties,
As experiences to prove,
When God has provided
Answers for our improve.

I hate many ways
Now amid life's ways,
But beauty is around us,
Thank God, for nature's ways.

E M Jones

Constellations

I do not want the constellations
          any nearer
They are very well where they are!
The nearer one reaches the zenith
          the further it is to fall.
Give me the lower pastures where the grass
          grows green and lush
And the rain falls and the wind blows;
          Where the pace of life is slower,
And there is no wild rush and mad frenetic raging.

For I have known the constellations
And have plumbed the greatest depths.
From the oceans to the heavens
          have I spanned -
And stood on the earth's crest,
There is much to be said to be
          as the fallow field,
To take in the scene all about me -
          and not to yield
To the cries of the world about me
In the heavens or the earth beneath
And hibernate and be free
Of this world's petty grind, its trivialities,
Of petty rules and regulations, of bureaucratic
          interference,
Of conflict and frustration, of VAT and tax!

There is much to be said for viewing
          the constellations
From earth's telescope instead,
As one views the triumphs and disasters
          on the television screen
While one takes of one's simple repast.

Patricia Florence Arnett

The Evils Of Smoking

Why oh why do mums smoke?
this habit should be stopped.
Smoking causes many serious
illnesses, and a danger of fires.

Good health should be top priority
at any age, life then can
Be enjoyed without personal
dangers to their children.

Nothing annoys me more
than to see a mum pushing a pram
With a cigarette stuck in her mouth.
they have no sense of responsibility.

I just cannot accept smoking.
a house full of smoke
Is ghastly, the rooms smell
stale and one cannot breathe.

The other side of this problem
is, instead of buying cigarettes,
Place the money for purchase
into a box, and take a holiday instead.

Mollie Elborough

Get Sorted

Uncle and Auntie
Stop gossiping about
others.

Look at your own
life and sort it
out.

Your boy has gone
and the girl on
the pill.

Get a life before
it is too late.

Bav

LOTTERY FEVER

Lottery fever makes my blood boil!
After a lifetime of scrimping and toil
To save for old age, no burden to be,
They take all *our* savings, our house
and its key!
Though we have bought them by going without,
Owing to no-one, one penny nor clout!

Yet this greedy machine they've set up of late
Gobbles up millions arranged by the State;
Supposedly helping to bring about good,
It's forgetting the charities, to help them it should!
While they spend on museums and places of art,
To hold a few pictures, some busts and a chart,
We're being pestered most every day
For large money sums, from our pensions to pay!

They're begging and pleading, because they're so short;
By emotional blackmail, we're nigh sent distraught!
'There's only *you* to put things to right;
We need lots of money, so send some *tonight!*
Or, better still, debit your monthly account;
That way, our problems, we'll maybe surmount!'

While we learn of millions, from papers and screen,
To go to the few, we think it's obscene
While millions are needed for problems so many;
Too much going to One, who won't spare a penny!
What kind of country fritters money away,
Allotting millions to one, despite the decay
Going on in the country, 'mongst thousands around,
Whose need is so great, yet nought is found?

What sort of person is begot of such greed,
That will grab all that's going, despite others' need?

Bee Wickens

Anger

I can tolerate many things, but what gets up my back
'tis the scum of our society, such people I cannot hack,
Those who go out of their way, just to break the law,
As each day passes by, we find there's more and more.

We get the mindless morons, who take great delight
of tipping rubbish in lay-bys, what a ghastly sight!
Little is done to deter them, as they ruin the countryside,
of what was once Great Britain, when folk took a bit of pride.

Alas those days have long-gone, we have a different race,
many have no pride at all, leaving trash all over the place,
Most of them are cowards, that's why they act at night,
thinking if they are not seen, everything will be alright.

Rapists and murderers, how they make my blood boil,
they should be made to suffer, chained and made to toil,
Sadly that is not the way, the criminal serves some time,
in a cell with all the trappings, and good food when they dine.

All criminals should be locked away, made to suffer every day,
they should sleep on wooden boards, covered with a little hay,
Their victims never had a choice, they had to take what came,
that's what puts my back up; criminals should suffer the same.

Wenn The Penn

Shoppers

A shopper is someone who goes to the shop.
No, that definition is wrong.
A shopper's a basket on wheels, very tall,
With a handle, one pulls it along

As one goes to the shop; it is dangerous too.
It is not pushed along like a pram
Or a pushchair or wheelbarrow but always is pulled.
I have seen many a 'shopper-jam'.

Someone with a shopper is like a road hog.
She comes out of the shop with her 'wheels'
And the person behind nearly trips over it.
What terrible anguish she feels.

For it's not 'Are you all right?' but 'You silly fool!'
And the shopper is pulled on its way,
While the victim checks over her parcels, herself
And her bag, to go shopping today.

Jillian Mounter

Double Glazing

'Hello, I'm selling windows,
Perhaps you've seen our ad.
We're round your area at present,
We can give you a quote that's not bad.

You're probably not thinking of windows right now
But what about next year?
The quote will still hold good then,
I don't think you'll find it too dear.'

No matter how much I tell them
I'm happy with the windows I've got,
Apart from the fact I can't afford it,
A few thousand to spare, I have not.

To be able to afford new windows one day
Would certainly be grand,
But my answer to the salesman has to be
'What part of 'no' don't you understand?'

But they never take 'no' for an answer,
Just keep up their chat - and how!
If they're not at the door being pushy
They'll ring me at tea-time I'll vow.

I must make up some early warning
So I don't have to answer the door.
Or some flashing light attached to the 'phone
That says 'windows' - there should be a law!

Barbara Brannigan

The Dreaded Queue

All I wanted was a bottle of wine,
Just to take home for when I dine,
But what met my eyes was sheer disbelief,
Supermarket trolleys bursting from beneath.

I raced for a gap, clutching my wine,
I need not have bothered, too late in line,
Back to the end of the queue I retreated,
Feeling downcast, dejected, defeated!

It seemed like a lifetime as I waited in vain.
It could have been worse, had I bought champagne,
What the hell I thought, don't feel so glum.
I could shout 'Fire!' and watch them run.

To pass off the boredom I pulled funny faces
At all those with full trolleys as if at the races.
'Come on my son,' I called at this young kid!
Perched on a trolley going into a skid.

I got to the checkout at last in a tizz,
My bottle of wine looked more like flat fizz,
'Ain't you got nuffin' smaller?' the cashier screamed . . .
Was this all for real . . . or just a bad dream?

Michael John Swain

PAPER CRIME

No friends write a letter - they all use the phone
The postman however never leaves me alone
He comes up with just armfuls to shove through my door
Mail piles up in heapfuls all over the floor.
Ask for a catalogue then receive three
Tick the square which says *'No more!'*
Yes, I know - it's all free.

Tons arrive in from all over the globe
Questionnaires, surveys, your lifestyle to probe
Are you married or single, detached or a flat?
Do you eat chocolate, have a dog or a cat?
Drive, smoke or drink, please answer all that.
Lotteries, bingo, scratch cards - the *Big Win*
You have won thousands by a flick of the wrist.
It's *you!* Yes it's *You* - but then comes the twist
First send twenty pounds - now I'm wearing a grin.

You must have, you need, every book, dress, CD
For over ten pounds you receive something free
A glittery bauble or some plastic clock.
Whatever it is you will get quite a shock.
Hold onto your money and always keep cool.
I'm beginning to think someone thinks I'm a fool.

I place the week's mail in a large plastic sack
Someone is paid to take it all back.
My patience I find is now just wearing thin
Reading the rubbish then having to bin.
What a terrible waste of one's life and one's time
People are paid for this paper-chase crime.

Pamela Estelle Gibson

NEW LABOUR, NEW BRITISH JUSTICE

British justice has a problem
For we can't afford a trial
With juries an extravagance
For the guilty in denial

Witnesses for the defence
Are such a waste of time
It's cheaper if we just convict
Those folk accused of crime

A judge could hear the evidence
Decide what should be done
Dispense with lawyers for defence
And Legal Aid grant none

The probation service could be cut
And prison staff could too
We could just dish out one sentence
For which hanging ought to do.

Kim Montia

THE FOX GLOWED

The fox glowed
his coat signed red gold
by the author of life.
His tail flicked
in the narrow breeze
as a truck passed
his corpse on the road.

Chris Moat

UNTITLED

We were not heroes
But innocents
We held no rifle
We were like children
On a beach.
Blue skies, lagoons, paradise
The island was beautiful
The sea full of life
Colourful rainbow fish
Tropical splendour.

We were not heroes
But innocent
We were like children
On a beach.
The skies filled with fire
The sea full of death
Paradise gone
Rainbow fish
Flotsam . . . stilled.

We were not heroes
But children.
Awed . . . mute . . . silenced.
And then the rain.
God bless the silenced few.
They were not heroes
But the innocent.

G J Hutchings

To News Hounds

The newspapers on sale today
Are full of horrors - but they say -
And this is what makes us so sad -
It is not news unless it's bad.

Unless the tale can catch your eye
And cause a heavy, heartfelt sigh
Or titillating sensual thrill
The newspapers will never sell.

One asks oneself 'Can this be so?'
Has humankind now sunk so low
That all it cares about is sin
Regardless of the voice within?'

When I recall the folk I knew
I cannot think that this is true
For in their lives they understood
Each act affects another's good.

Can we not have, before too late,
Some better news to contemplate?
As well as wars and actions dire
Please give us something to inspire.

Evelyn Westwood

THE SHOPPING LIST

Granary bread,
Cheese and ham,
Packet of biscuits,
Tin of Spam!
Loo rolls - pink - extra-soft,
Clearasil - that's facial wash,
Two tins of beans,
Four packs of lager,
Frozen peas,
Disprin for the 'morning after'!
Vanilla ice-cream,
Uncut loaf,
Jacob's crackers and melba toast,
Sweets for Becky,
Yoghurt for Paul,
Amy asked for cotton wool -
Joint for Sunday,
Lamb or pork
Butter for spreading
2 lbs of Stork.
Pastry - frozen
Squash and juice
3 lbs of plums - I prefer them loose,
A couple of apples
A sticky bun,
TV guide, copy of 'The Sun'
Treat for Mummy
Yes- that'll do
Now I'll wait half an hour,
To battle the queue!

K Lawrence

The Modern-Day Sin

What is this feeling? What is this pain?
constant and numbing, over and over again.
The thrumming and drumming of cars on the roads,
a screech of some brakes and your mind overloads.
The overhead roar of planes by the score
crashes into your conscious and is hard to ignore.

Nerve-jarring road drills bore into your head,
by the time you reach work you wish you were dead.
Trains trundle and clatter in station and siding,
your heart's pumping wildly, you're full of foreboding.
The stale frowzy stench of the city decay
just fills me with sadness, alarm and dismay.

Factory chimneys spew death in laden-grey plumes
and the air hangs heavy with the dirt and the fumes.
Birdsong is drowned under the immutable din
of the hustle and bustle of this modern-day sin.
Muddled and smothered is all thought and reason
by the frenzy of voices no longer in unison.

Why isn't there peace and quiet anymore?
quiescence and tranquillity will be nevermore.
Lost is man's youth, misplaced our spare time,
it's just stresses and strains and the festering grime.
The air is polluted, the oceans are dying,
so how much longer can life go on surviving?

Jean Selmes

ORGANISED CHAOS

Absolute chaos wae cars everywhere,
Wae lanes jist fur buses, oh an' taxis as well.
They call themselves 'planners' but aw' ah can see
Is ah could dae better wi'oot a degree.

A better description - jist 'man designed'
An no very weel - but it's aw' in their mind.
They call it 'road management' but that's jist a joke.
A much better bargain wi' pigs in a poke.

Whit a wid sae is - gee us a break.
Let's jist enjoy life for goodness sake.
Oor time's short enough wi'oot aw' this hassle
Must we jist stay at hame and prove it's oor castle?

Naw - ah'm no givin' in tae their bullying tactics
Where ah go, ma car goes tae.
Ah'm no payin' dues tae leave it at hame
If the rest are as wise, they'll aw' dae the same.

Agnes Bruce

The Chase

There they go the baying hounds,
to the sound of the hunting horn.
The well-dressed band of riders,
on a cold and frosty morn.

The chase is on, the quarry's spotted,
the orders given, off they go.
Horses snorting, riders urging,
voices calling, 'Tally Ho.'

Spread across the grassy meadows,
the thirsting pack are in full flow.
Closely followed by the Master,
cracking whip, his face aglow.

The tired fox is slowing quickly,
fierce dogs are closing fast.
Pouncing on the helpless creature,
people watching all aghast.

The gruesome chase is over,
the deadly deal is done.
The breathless cruel huntsmen,
have had their slice of fun.

Alwyn James

JOKERS

What is it about Golf GTIs
that they have to take me by total surprise?

In '89 the culprit was red
and landed me in a hospital bed.

This one was dark blue . . .
and in seven days my holiday was due.

An ordinary, everyday post office trip
suddenly changed to a cartoon strip.

Engrossed in my handbag search
I totally ignored the other car's perch.

Sans driver, higher up the hill
and due to take an unscheduled spill.

So silently, it rolled, gathering speed,
with only my car its jaunt to impede.

Leaving a handbrake off is bad enough.
Only caring for car welfare is really tough.

This isn't Tom and Jerry or Scooby-Doo . . .
I don't bounce back unscathed in Scene Two.

So, all you jokers out there, alias Golf GTIs:
I've got your number - so watch out guys!

Christine Thomas

THE ANGRY NURSE

My house-bound patients' lives are run
Round programmes on TV.
They can't enjoy the summer sun,
They have to wait for me.

The TV is their only link
With what goes on outside.
Their programmes also make them think
As they take life in their stride.

When schools break up for holidays
Their pleasures cease to matter
And for many weeks, not just for days
Their screen shows children's clatter.

The children can go out to play
And usually they do.
My patients spend a boring day
Why should it happen so?

The people trapped within their home
Will pay their licence too
While children freely run and roam
I think it's wrong don't you?

Not only does it seem so wrong
But it is insulting too.
Bodies may be weak but minds are strong
TV producers, think this through.

If your day was spent sat in a chair,
Maybe laid upon a bed,
You'd change your mind and have a care
Put important programmes on instead.

Frieda Cox

Imperious Bird

Imperious bird
Haven't you heard
The reports put about?
They say you're a lout
On the streets; scattering
The trash; splattering
Our windows and cars;
That your course repertoires
From rooftop nests,
Shatter endeavours to catch up on rest;
And that your scouts always know
When we dine al fresco,
Swooping to snatch tasty snacks from the hand
With all the finesse of a common brigand.

So scavenger bird
We'll have the last word;
For plans are afoot
To give you the boot,
Back to the fields, the headlands, the sea,
And survival that comes without guarantee.

C Baudains

Smothered - A Steady Heartbeat

Hitting the highs
Hitting the lows and all the walls in-between.
Welcome to fat land.
Floating in the fat and easy pool
Where smiles become boring,
snide,
and then scary.
Welcome to steady world
getting fat and easy
sleazy and wheezy
from too much sitting around.
Everyone stops reaching and falling
there's no more flying
and there's no more crawling
Only a feeling, censored and obscene
A steady heartbeat.

J Kidd

FORWARD OR BACKWARD

For modern day laundry
New-fangled machine,
Everything automatic
To wash, dry and clean.
But clothes manufacturers
Don't seem to know that,
The instructions say
Hand wash and dry flat!

Catherine Langdon

DISGUSTING

What gets my back up?
These people, who write to newspapers to complain,
All read the letters of complainants,
Full of rage and bitterness, on the letter page.
Someone prints them for a wage,
All read the yup.

All in cars, taking the pressure off their feet,
No coppers on the beat,
In our street.
How disgusting, an old throw away toilet seat.
A throw away throne from some one home.
And a lot more, heaps of rubbish left to rot.

Dangerous cycleways,
Full of parked vehicles, potholes and drains,
Where's the brains?
What's the price of two white lines?
On sidewalks
Where only a few people walk.

Down at heel houses in parts of our town;
Run down, repairs don't get done!
Are these our future shanty towns?
Who cares about the young.
Dogs' muck in our streets,
That stick to our feet.

On people advice
Write about the nice things in life,
Don't think that's right, how disgusting
Letters go on, postman's bag must weigh a ton.
Must do something about the complaints
I must stop writing them, I the one.

Bryan Clarke

Put Downs

There must be a school I don't know about that teaches people
to be rude
How to turn an innocent remark with a twist, to something crude.
How to embarrass and humiliate, leaving one subdued.

Not that I want to go to it, I'd hate to learn the skill -
But I'd like to know well in advance how they step in for the kill
And to take avoiding action. I'd like to know the drill.

Naively, I know I ask for it, step in with two left feet,
And their quick sarcastic put downs are clever and complete
And even though the laugh's on me, I admit their reposte is neat.

But when I am shy and ill at ease, dispirited, down, or low,
They take away my confidence, and deal a dirty blow.
They think they are the greatest clowns, with their tee-hee and ho ho!

Don't they realise how much it hurts when they smirk and sneer?
It may make them feel better, more superior to jeer.
But to score a point on little me is no big deal, I fear.

If the only way they can feel good is to put down and deride
Some other human being and regard the act with pride,
I wonder why they need it and how they feel inside.

Sometimes their remarks are below the belt and so untrue, they shock
And I can reply in nasty kind and bear brunt of their knock.
I can answer back and cap them on some other soul's behalf,
And turn it so that in the end it's us who get last laugh.
But I hate the silly grin they give to offset their nasty crack
Just in case you take offence and demand they take it back.
Their smirks just go to prove to me, they are proud of their attack.

So I give them marks 10 out of 10 graduated from this school
That I don't know about, they are nobody's fool,
But I've learnt to turn the other cheek, pretend to play it cool
And retaliate their superior smirk with a sneer of ridicule.
This makes *me* feel as bad as *them,* ungracious at their 'joke'
But they are so supercilious and smug, their taunts in me evoke
Uncharacteristic tendencies to give their eye a poke!

Beryl Ward

STUBBLE TROUBLE

I must admit I'm quite content
To see hair growing where it's meant
Sometimes alas hair may begin
To grow upon a female chin
The sight of this both sparse or thick
Can make me absolutely sick.
There is a cure without a doubt
So ladies tweeze the last one out
And you will never more offend
You husband, partner or a friend.

Mary Rea

Holy Innocents Of The Twentieth Century

Oh, never since the world began, has such a sight been seen!

Unprecedented is this flood,
The victims of cruel death,
Cut off like flowers in the bud
Before they could draw breath.

And still they come, the nameless hosts,
While Heaven stands aghast
To see the tiny homeless ghosts;
To welcome them at last.

These holy innocents who saw
Not sun, nor moon, nor rain,
Nor parents' smiles, knew only raw
Extinguishment in pain.

Despised, rejected, bloody, torn,
Discarded in a bin,
No mother ever wished them born,
But *they* are free from sin.

Aborted foetuses who at
Conception gained your soul,
Come now to Jesus knowing that
His love will make you whole.

This Man of Sorrows no more dies,
The victim of man's strife.
He'll smile into your cold, lost eyes
And warm you into Life.

Then pass you to the loving care
Of those who were not given
On earth a child, who wept in prayer:
You fill their joy in Heaven.

Audrey Turner

People Who Do Not Really Understand

You look at me as I try to explain
What has happened to me
It really is quite simple
Why can't you seem to see.

My life may look easy
To you on the outside
But deep down I have
A great deal of pain inside.

I know you mean well
As you gently take my hand
But how can you really
Ever truly understand.

I may be in a wheelchair
But I am not totally useless
And I wish that you were honest
Enough to simply address.

That you do not really understand
The patronising way that you act
Could sometimes be handled
With just a bit more tact.

Ian Fowler

To Gripe And Moan

In life we have to gripe and moan
The price of calls
The telephone
The state of our banks
Interest rate
The cost of what
It costs to pay
The water rates
Our income tax
We love to gripe
Of this and that
It doesn't change
A bloomin' thing
We need to grumble
That's the thing
And at the end
Of a long day's graft
We share a long cold beer
At last
What a scandalous price for beer
Everything is flippin' dear
So now we gripe and moan again
Where is all this going to end?

Jeanette Gaffney

THE IGNORANT GENERATION

Medals hang upon the elders' lapels
glimmering in the spring sunshine,
enhancing the glow of amazement.
Precious survival.
Glory long past,
dragged back from the dead,
for torturous nostalgia.
Boasts of heroism fall on deaf ears.

We are the ignorant generation.

Scorn adorns as rambling stories dominate,
uttered from drunken lips.
Our disbelief reigns.
The fragile skeletons
know nothing, only lost comrades,
forgotten sweethearts,
and the sound of guns in their heads at nights.

Yet the poppies are only flowers,
the medals only metal
and the graves only stones.

We are the ignorant generation.

Gemma Bowen

THE DECEITFUL LOVER

Dissatisfied with 'just' love, you wanted worship.
The greed you breathed would not allow me self esteem;
Arrogance exuded sneered at my deep beliefs -
The selfishness you bore scorned all my dreams.

You lapped up all the attention, basked in my courtship;
Deceit in every thought and deed, lies in your eyes,
You laughed behind my back, you gifted only grief -
With twisted glee, my heart you cauterised.

No hideous torment could match the pain inside,
No chemical sear vitals like your rejection.
Nothing burns within like the knowledge you were false;
Nothing drags me down like this dejection.

No anger rivals fury of despair with hindsight,
No grudge fades slower than that born of injustice!
No wrong of man nor beast can speed the vengeful pulse
Like lover whom worthy of distrust is.

Phoenix Martin

MAN'S INFLICTIONS

Man inflicts sorrow
Man inflicts pain
there's no tomorrow
when hate turns insane

Man inflicts terror
Man inflicts horror
Man inflicts tremor
when lacking human glamour

Man inflicts atrocities
Man commits ferocities
Man enacts brutality
When seized by abnormality

Man has to improve his ways
get human and behave with grace
then, maybe, Man will enjoy
his short life filled with joy

Wila Yagel

Customers

When employed by a shop
you are there to serve
but goodness me some customers
really have a nerve.
They tell of their aches and pains
and how it isn't fair
they tell you of their holidays
like you're supposed to care.
They moan about the prices
they moan about the queue
they moan about the weather
and they take it out on you.
So when you're doing your shopping
wherever you may be
spare a thought for the staff
who knows, it could be me.

Joy Benford

For Love Or Money

Infuriation and irritation,
My blood pressure ready to blow.
When yet another attack on animals,
On the news is shown.

The slaughter of the white seal pups,
What chance do they stand?
If the poachers want their coats so much,
Then why don't they grow their own.

The hunting of the deer and fox,
A nation of animal lovers be damned.
If we really had a conscience,
Then we would *all* demand a ban.

Chasing the beautiful innocent creatures,
We should all admire and enjoy.
Be proud of our English countryside,
And not go out and destroy.

It makes me so so angry,
When animals are given as gifts.
Everyone knows a puppy grows up,
Now I'm really getting miffed.

These horror stories you're always hearing,
Charities pleading for help.
Yes, I know they ask for donations,
But it's out of animal love.

Alright I know my bleating,
Won't change anything I've said.
But isn't it about time someone listened,
Before it really becomes all too late.

Audra Ann Murphy

Mad Passionate Love

I love Noel Edmunds, I love mobile phones,
And flag-days, Rolf Harris and motorway cones,
And faxes, and wheel-clamps, and washing my hair,
And car alarms, health farms, and Prescott and Blair,
Love people with clipboards who won't let you move,
Who ask if your sex life might ever improve,
And I love spending hours in Post Office queues,
While punters with scratch cards blaspheme as they lose,
I think that those fellows are simply amazing
Who phone during teatime and sell double glazing,
And when all that marvellous sales talk is over,
I love all those Witnesses sent by Jehovah,
I love Ecstasy tablets, and ice-cream van chimes,
And leaflets tucked into the Radio Times,
I love all those switchbacks that make me feel queasy,
And manuals that tell me computers are easy,
I love Karaoke, a pub with a quiz,
And Charles and Camilla, and Philip and Liz,
That psychiatrist chappie, I simply adored,
And I love all the people I see on the ward,
I love all the nurses, they're gentle with me,
And they say when I'm cured, they'll let me go free!

Peter Davies

THEY SAID

They,
They said,
'It couldn't happen,'
Then they said,
'It didn't.'
I mean, 'the six million'.
The wiping out of,
Them, the unrested ones
Of concentration camp horrors,
And gas chamber piles
Of sickening, 'final solution',
But then,
What was the question?
Was it in the countless books of yesterday,
The counting of the endless bodies after,
All under the same silent sky?
And did God look on,
From a distant thunder?
Without,
Even striking the faintest light,
For the burning days of men;
As he heard then,
As he hears of now, the words;
'That, *they* just couldn't count the numbers,
Oh! No, they couldn't
Of all those,
Who just looked the other way.'
They said,
They.

Norman Royal

THE JOB CENTRE

You've joined the millions unemployed, so what must you do?
Go to the nearest Job Centre and wait there in the queue
At last you're at the counter - but then what do you find?
You get a booklet to fill in to bring back another time!
The forms you had are now complete so off you go again
You had to walk - you've got no fare, so hope it doesn't rain.
Standing once again in line the minutes ticking past
It takes nearly an hour, then it's your turn at last.
You have to lose the first three days because that is the law,
Something you did not know about never signing on before!
The Giro should be sent to you within the next two days
You walk back home so slowly, your mind is in a daze.
You sign on with an agency, perhaps they may have work
From this occupation, you never tried to shirk.
The telephone is ringing, 'Can you work next week?'
Of course the answer must be yes - so now you must speak
To the people at the Job Centre again - you need *another* form
This work must be declared for this is now the norm.
The work is done the form filled in, you're in the queue once more
But when you reach the counter, there is a shock in store.
Because you worked a week your claim has been closed down
Something you can't understand, so you look and frown
You must fill in these *other forms*, is what you are now told
No more can people work a week and declare, as they did of old.
It really isn't worth it, to earn just one week's pay,
You lose two weeks' unemployment -
So from now on home you'll stay.
There's really no incentive - temping's not the thing to do
When it means you pay for working - when they should be paying you!

Letitia Snow

A Hymn Of Hate

Were I a happy natured bloke,
respected and beloved of folk,
I'd always wear a happy smile
and think contented thoughts the while.

The facts, however, aren't like that,
I am a peevish geriat -
ric, rude, morose, of language foul
and wearing a perpetual scowl.

The list of all that I detest
is long, and so I thought it best
to mention just one violent hate -
that most un-English word 'donate'.

I'll curse as long as I may live
those who 'donate' when meaning 'give'.
(Why use two syllables, I ask,
when one performs a better task?)

Occasionally (though I confess
it's rare) I think I may be less
than right. However, in this case
no reappraisal can take place.

So, should I meet some person who,
perversely, takes a different view,
I'll gladly, should it come to blows,
donate him one upon the nose.

Martin Summers

DEMOCRACY?

In a democratic country, such as ours,
Ever the cry 'Roads are jammed, we need another.'
Which faceless ones, give their little men, such powers -
Who is going to stop the bureaucrats' take-over?

Democracy, we are told, is fairness to all,
What's fair about the onslaught of a bulldozer,
Smashing a home, to each occupant, special -
A happy family caring for each other?

Equal, politically and socially -
Principles of democracy, but absent here,
Where generations have toiled, stoically,
There's a new motorway, where their corn waved last year!

'We're only doing our job,' the bailiffs stated,
Puffed up officials, ran round like frightened mice.
Protesters moved out - overlords elated,
With not a thought given, to those who paid the price!

Elizabeth Harris

The Honorary Degree

I don't need to sit and think, my dear,
What gets my back up today:
It's the 'Honorary Degree', without a doubt,
That I have plenty to say.

When I see them in the newspaper,
Or on the television screen:
Climbing up on the platform, so pleased -
With themselves - I could surely scream.

Many years ago, twenty to be exact,
I decided - a degree, is what I should do.
It took tremendous effort - work ever treble checked.
Not easy, but I did it, at the age of fifty two.

So maybe someone can see my point,
A school to run, a family of three to feed,
Then I see them given for football, acting, sculpture,
Well paid occupations without a degree - yes indeed.

I know there's nothing can be done,
I'm satisfied - I did my best.
I'm very proud of all my work,
But it gets the moaning off my chest.

Dorothy Whitehall

I Love My Neighbours - But

I am *not* normally a jealous person - but
My neighbour goes regularly to *Twickenham* - to watch *rugger,*
And - as I cannot bring myself, to mention his name
Just refer to him, as *'that lucky bugger'*.

I am *not* normally a jealous person - but
It *hurt* - when a junior colleague at work - received promotion,
Tomorrow - it's my turn - to pour the afternoon tea
I am seriously thinking of mixing - a potion.

I am *not* normally a jealous person - but
I hated *Mr Brown* - when he bought that *new car,*
And further - as my *wife* is somewhat flat-chested
She hates *Mrs Brown* - who wears a *larger size* bra.

I am *not* normally a jealous person - but
Those at number 8 - every winter - go *skiing* abroad,
Naturally, I don't wish them any harm, but
If there *were* an *accident* - I wouldn't fail, to visit their
hospital ward.

I am *not* a normally jealous person - but
That chap next door, is so handsome - he is turning my wife's head,
She worships and treats him - like *royalty*
So I wonder - is he better than me - *in bed?*

Paul Gold

Drifting

Why do you drift from the quay
of your belonging?
The harbour lights grow dim from
your divide;
What is the shadow of your disquiet?
Is it that you build your world
beyond void horizons?
Do you not see that we too have
a wanting?

What will you see when you arrive
at your final dawn?
Will you again keep your distance?
What will you expect of your carer?
What will your carer expect of you?

Peter Morriss

INFORMATION

The bag informs us, in four languages
how much to use, how long it should last,
safety instructions, hand rinsing instructions,
how to receive, a not so eco-friendly sphere
enabling us, to use the product.
(How did we ever manage?)
Idiot proof, in four languages!
Euro-manufacturers now decline, to include
the only missing piece of the multi-lingual
information jigsaw, the one housewives would term,
really useful!
Precisely which fabrics may we use the product for?
(In four languages?)

Jacquie L Smith

I LOVE BARBIE, BY DADDY!

In my house we've a box for Barbie toys
Barbies strewn across the floor and causing lots of noise.

There's a Barbie on my breakfast, in the butter for my toast
There's a Barbie in the oven, helping with the Sunday roast.

There's a Barbie up the Hoover, having trodden on the stair
There's a Barbie in my briefcase, who has lost her underwear.

In my house there's a Barbie on the phone
Giving Ken an ear-bashing in no uncertain tone.

There's a Barbie filming Baywatch that young Ken has come to meet
With a kiss and cuddle make up in the back seat of their jeep.

There's a Barbie getting married, yes, that's bound to cause a scene
While Sindy's nose is out of joint, a Play-Doh shade of green.

We've accessories for this and that, a hundred kinds of shoe
With Shelly in her pushchair, having toppled down the loo.

There's a Barbie in the bathroom trying to wax her underarm
Using Daddy's razor blade, I mustn't show alarm!

There's a Barbie on my duvet when I'm getting into bed
When I wake up in the morning, the dog's bitten off her head.

In my house Barbies are banned!
Then I hear a whingeing child, 'Daddy just doesn't understand!'

Chris Roy Smith

The Create Debate

A visit to the Tate Gallery has,
Convinced me that art is dead,
The artists who brought us beauty and joy,
Are extinct and regrettably fled.
Tradition is now outdated,
A past impossible law,
Succeeded with cold arrogance,
By a meaningless mindless bore.
I felt cheated and shocked,
When I saw this display,
I love beauty and art,
The traditional way.
Go back to artistry,
That comes from the heart,
The Tate may be modern,
But don't call it art.

Brian O'Brien

LEGAL VANDALS

The fields once peacefully were seen
Covering the land with green;
Farm hands worked to raise the crops
Needed to supply our shops.

Wild flowers grew in great profusion;
Animals lived without confusion;
Rabbits, hares and harvest mice
Prospered in this paradise.

Time came when the greed of man
Caused the forming of a plan
To strip the fields and lay them bare;
Instead - build houses everywhere.

So one day in bleak November
Came a day we'll all remember;
To the fields, instead of tractors
Came machines of the contractors.

Stakes and ropes marked out the land;
JCBs moved in as planned:
The legal vandals of our day
Had come to take our peace away.

Geoff Tullett

Let There Be Light

I am close to desperation
Thanks to a neighbour's illuminations
His beloved security light
Keeps me awake at night
E'er a leaf passes by
It shines straight at my eyes
I try to turn my back
But the darkness I do lack
And when the car parks in the drive
The light, it comes alive
Thanks to its microchip brain
I am dazzled once again
Add in a streetlight's amber glow
And can I sleep? No.
The city is so bright
I miss that wondrous sight
Of the jewelled canopy of stars
Or even the red planet Mars
But does it help security?
No, *our* burglars it did not see.

Andrew Fisher

End It!

Pebbles, all shapes and sizes, glisten in the powdery sand,
Nature's bounty washed up from the crystal sea.
Yet, here at tide line, in such profusion,
Something mars the beauty the eye can see!

Cigarette ends! Tell-tale signs of Man's addiction,
Saliva-contaminated butts thrown at will.
No thought for others' seaside pleasure
As long as he has puffed his fill.

Dirty, mouth-sucked ends of nicotined paper
Discarded selfishly where Man has stayed,
Left amongst enticing shells and pebbles
Where children play with bucket and spade.

Why must Man flaunt this filthy habit?
Is it not enough he's killing himself?
That he has to spread oral infection
Tainting the children and risking their health!

Pat Heppel

ANNOYING

There are certain words in the English language
That some of us seem to have difficulty pronouncing
Why this is I do not know -
Even taking account of local dialects.
Media presenters and newsreaders do it
And I just thought they would know better.
But the word that annoys me most
Is the pronunciation of B - double E - N
Why, oh why, do people say 'bin'?
Had you not noticed? Well you just listen
And I am sure before one day is through
Many times 'been' as in 'seen'
Will have become 'bin' as in 'sin'.

Mary A Slater

DOGGIE DO'S

In the open they walk the paths that spread across the land,
To take the air and steal the scenes of rural England.
By their side a companion, their pal,
Sharing every path, marking every trail.
Each track cut through fields of green
The evidence of every step they've been,
And those who follow in their wake
To take the view, make this mistake
Of not watching the ground they tread
And stepping in doggie do's instead.
Packets left for all to share,
To tread and spread and curse and swear
As they take in the country air,
And as they pass the doggie bins a pile will lay below,
Obviously the bin's too high for the dog to sit and go.

Colin Farmer

A Dominie's Lament

Once upon a time,
When knowledge was prized,
Classroom learning was cerebral,
And uniquely interpersonal,
A teacher-fed
Nurturing of the mind.

Founded upon sound reason,
Rote, and repetition,
Word and number mastery
Had direction,
A competence for all seasons,
Enduring as life itself.

Until, that is, the dawning
Of our new electronic age
Spawned computers en masse,
Dehumanising scholarly exchange,
And short-circuiting
The dominie as trusty sage.

As a modern tool
For the traditional chalkface,
The computer soon commandeered space
At the curriculum core,
Creating yet another role for school
As a disc-led hardware store.

A trickle of technology
Fast escalating into a tidal bore
That now swamps work and play,
And casts even adult minds
Adrift upon a sea of digitised
Data, stranded far from shore.

Andrew Farmer

Rep Life

A company car and mobile phone,
a clean white shirt and brand new home.
A smiling wife and well behaved kids,
just meet your target and that's how you can live.

Be wanton and greedy and always agree,
then you can be happy, be top of the tree.
You might win a holiday or brand new car
you could get promoted and really go far.

Don't ever ask about life and its meaning
as the answers are there with the sales you're receiving.
In the evening ring some of your friends
why there's that bloke you sold loads to just last weekend.

Then take your plastic to buy a cheap bottle of wine
to look at your family without smiling sublime.
Watch a video all about life
and get up in the morning as sharp as a knife.

Nick Carlon

PLEASE SCOOP YOUR DOG'S POOP!

You should buy a mog,
Instead of a dog,
If it causes you stress,
To clear up its mess!

Don't leave it there,
Without a care,
But use a scoop,
To remove its poop!

Squirming worms,
And lots of germs,
Make their nests,
In dogs' mess!

It could make us ill,
Much worse than a chill,
So please be strong,
And remove that *stinking pong!*

C Shadwell

The Fence Sitter

The fence-sitter is not
my flavour of the year,
he never lets his thoughts be known
his views are never clear.

He would make a decision
and it wouldn't hurt his pride,
providing when he jumped
he landed on the winning side.

But he can't take the chance,
like Humpty - sits upon the wall,
for it is so much easier
not to make a choice at all.

He won't ever nail his colours
to the mast - and that's the crunch,
yes, the fence sitter must be
the 'nana of the bunch.

Fay Smith

A Pensioner's Lament

I look at the way they live today
I don't understand what they have to say
I can't see why they dress that way
With shaven heads and painted faces
They dance like natives around a 'pot'
And take their pills to cure 'what'
They expect we others to be happy to pay
To provide them with their needs for the day
But, expect them to pay 'their round' 'Oh nay'
It's always someone else whose caused it all
And it's they who should pay to meet their needs
That they may continue with their deeds
So
Were those lost years from 1914 onwards meant to be
So that we oldies can now keep alive
On pounds sixty five?

Richard W Archard

A Bad Habit

I hate when people light cigarettes,
Then blow smoke in your face,
They don't think they're doing wrong,
But I think it's a disgrace.

The thought of getting lung cancer,
Doesn't seem to bother some folk,
But for non-smokers, to breath in their smoke all day,
Is certainly not a joke.

Now most smokers who enjoy the bad habit,
Will end up using a 'puffer',
But in the meantime they should make sure,
That other people do not suffer.

Jean Hendrie

To Wear His Ring

The rent ain't been paid there's no coal in the shed
Electricity is running low
There's no cups in the rack they're all up by the bed
And now he's gone out to the show

Now the house is a mess but he's managed to score
A little Oxo to help him along
And the wine has been fine he's gonna have some more
It makes him feel so strong

He don't do the washing he don't cook the food
He don't do much of anything
He don't give a damn for the things that he should
Now he wants you to wear his ring

Wear his ring he wants to make you his own
He knows that you're afraid of the dark
Wear his ring he'll never leave you alone
But his bite is much worse than his bark

Michael Shimmin

A THOUGHT FOR OTHERS

Ill mannered people make me cross when in a queue we wait
When the bus arrives they infuriate me as to the front they skate.
Elderly people I feel sorry for when others surge and scurry
Hard of hearing, some cannot walk but no one seems to worry.
In order to alleviate this I try to stand between,
And as the queue hastens up front I squash in to be seen.
I often get shocking glances as in order I keep the queue
I also despise the way we treat each other,
As senior citizens are but a few.
So what does it take to wait awhile, to be courteous and kind
When after all we should care a little, and always keep this in mind.

Jean Calver

TALK

It's a funny old world we live in today
People talk about you come what may
There is nowhere you can go
To find a bit of peace you know
Some people do nothing but gossip about you
Which is nothing new
And even talk when they go to the loo.
You can't go away
Without them causing trouble
They always have their say
You even hear people talk to themselves
So keep what you know to yourself.

D McNeil

All Around Me

All around me I hear them say
'What do you do all day?'
It makes me want to cry
And here's why,
I cook and clean and sew
And take them where they have to go,
And when you come home to rest,
Why then I must prepare them for a test
Next day, and then I must get lunches,
(Tomorrow I'll do her hair in bunches)
'Where's my jeans?' I hear one say,
'Among the clothes I ironed today'
'My clothes are really terribly dirty,'
(I wish my eldest wouldn't get so 'shirty')
With me; after all this is really quite crazy
They all think I'm incredibly lazy.

Margaret Boles

A TIDY PLACE

Sweet wrappers
chip papers,
rubbish of every hue
old chewing gum that sticks onto my shoe.
Broken glass,
tins and cans that cannot pass
a litter bin
it's so easy you just chuck it in.
It makes me angry, it makes me sad,
why are some people's manners so bad?
A tidy place
makes a happy face.
Why can't you when goods are bought,
do as I was always taught
and take your rubbish home?

Rosemary Medland

Exist And Don't Let Live

Just look at you, you scruff.
We can spot you from afar
Easy to tell by your clothes, your hair,
Or even by your car.

A bunch of mindless football thugs,
Drink ten pints every night.
Then throw up a red-hot vindaloo,
In time for a gang fight.

And her, a tart, it's obvious.
Just look at how she's dressed.
The hussy should be soundly flogged,
She looks a bloody mess.

And look at them, they must be druggies
Hanging around those dodgy dives.
All of 'em stealing and dealing,
In our nice kiddies' little lives.

And another one over there!
Scruffy sod I do declare.
I bet that tramp's not had a bath,
Since the sodding midwife was there.

And me, I'm not a bigot,
Don't have that sort around here.
I just sit all sweet and ignorant
In judgement on you all.

Ivan S Cherry

The Redundant Ferryman

Sat in the shade, under an old gnarled tree.
Listening to the water of the gently flowing stream.
I close my eyes and fancy, it is talking to me,
Of when it was a river and how powerful it used to be.

The river watched the tree growing tall and strong,
Never thinking, he would be the weaker one.
As the years passed by, trees became protected.
You could not chop them down, unless they were infected.

You would not think, to look at me now,
I kept a waterwheel, turning round and round.
Scooped up at one side, tipped out at the other.
Me and the waterwheel, we had such fun together.

Then came the mills with automatic power.
I was a dumping ground, for their wasted matter.
It polluted the water and killed a lot of fish,
The people did not care, they were getting rich.

Those times were cruel but worse was yet to come,
With automatic power, the washing machine was born.
Followed by the dishwasher, to help the idle cope,
And what do they need to work, well water, of course.

A branch from the tree softly tapped me on the head,
It was shaking with laughter, at what the stream had said.
The stream carried on talking and ignored his old friend.
Who do they come to when the rain does not descend?

The waterboard came and piped me away,
No one protested, until it was too late.
I often feel angry, at the way they treated me
And sometimes I wish I could have been a tree.

Linda Tosney

Lest We . . . Forget

shrunken and stooped figures
bent by november's gusting
wind, aged, weary arthritic
limbs stand painfully defiant
in mothballed sunday best,
proud poppy on the chest.

sombre and sad they struggle
in ragged formation, trekking
towards the memorial cross,
marching ever nearer their
cherished long-lost loved ones,
and that final heavenly reunion.

faded berets, sacred medals
hang from frayed ribbons,
few now remain, kindred
comrades, faithful widows,
respectful diligent relatives.

proud but bitter, bewildered by
50 years of insignificant pensions
and benefits, meagre recognition
from successive, cynical governments
and un-elected, un-civil servants.

token gestures of memorial benches,
is
poor reward for death in the trenches . . .

John Hirst

A Hot Day

England's gentle springtime
Sets my heart a-glow,
Returning birds and flowers
wherever I may go.

But this still air, this burning heat,
Brings my spirit to a stop,
No water so birds and flowers gone
Lying dead at my feet.

Day after day the sky afire,
Sunrise and sunset never-ending,
More and more men and beast expire,
Earth obviously having its last fling.

Lord one last prayer,
Take my loved ones to your care,
Forgive man's foolishness,
Then I awoke, saw you standing there.

Florence Andrews

Bite Back

Love is lost when one can see,
Parents with their child.
'Behave Shirley,' says Mother,
Shirley looks up at her mum
Then giggles, she skips along
One can see the child scheming
For the moment when she
Can be naughty again!
Shirley can't wait to chastise
Her worried mother and father
Singing as she trips along pretends
To accidentally fall,
They comfort Shirley.
As I walk by I shake my head
She giggles with sheer delight!

Alma Montgomery Frank

WHAT TO HAVE?

Smoking causes cancer,
So the doctors say.
But life wouldn't be much fun,
If the authorities got their way.

Butter isn't good for us,
Puts our cholesterol high,
And if we don't watch the *E*s in food,
We'll be hyperactive by and by.

There's 'E-coli' in our meat,
Pesticides on our fruit.
Remember myxomatosis?
So rabbits we should shoot.

Mad-cow disease and botulism,
In fact I even dread
To think what happens when I eat
My ration of daily bread.

Too many eggs must be avoided,
In fact it's very plain,
If we listen to all they have to say,
We'd never eat again.

M Muirhead

Off The Rails

Points that have frozen
So trains cannot go -
The wrong kind of snow.

Rails that have buckled
So trains cannot run -
The wrong kind of sun.

Rails that are slippery
So trains cannot speed -
The wrong kind of leaves.

Whatever the weather,
We stand and wait -
The train's always late.

Geraldine Foy

GATHERING STORM

Let me show you a place where trees don't bend to the wind
because there are no trees.
Instead the wind gusts over derelict patches of weed-stricken
shopping trolleys, mattresses, broken washing machines
and other domestic detritus. It screams up alleyways fouled with
crisp packets, cigarette papers, plastic bags and spent condoms.
It buffets against broken swings, fractured slides and see-saws.
It brushes over syringes and splintered glass.
It howls about tower blocks, urine foetid lifts,
graffiti daubed stairwells and boarded windows.
It knocks against uneven pavements, deserted shops,
and discarded dustbins.
It fights with the wail of police sirens, the strident shrieking
from the ghetto-blasters, the raucous savagery of street mobs,
the dreary weeping of desperation, the tumbling violence of
drunken argument, the screech of stolen tyres,
the piercing cry in the darkness.

And it sobs, how it sobs, for the unemployed drifters,
the neglected children,
the battered, the bullied, the beaten, the weak and defenceless.
It moans for the hopelessness.
It shudders, it shivers, for the future.

Gillian Howarth

THE INNOCENT ONES

Tiny and fragile they do not try to escape
These poor animals have come to their fate
Locked in cages without a care, by people who are not being fair
Just for the greediness of mankind
Animals from all over the world they find
They torture and disfigure them without as much as a thought
I wonder how they would feel if it was their families
That were being caught.
These animals are the innocent victims, they have done no wrong
So they should be freed back into the wild where they belong.

Ann Grimwood

Beware!

Beware of the telephone
Could leave you with a moan
All the 'Mock'
'Good to talk'
Is for their gain
As always the game

My 'phone costs appeared high
I wondered why!
I kept check on each call
Which seem'd up the wall
When surveying the cost
I felt at a loss.

When 'bereaved' and 'alone'
One needs a friend on the 'phone
To lighten their grief
And bring to them peace
The reason my 'phone I did use
Giving comfort but also confuse

On checking their exorbitant price
I was filled with surprise
And so astonished!
I decided to abolish
My oh so 'dear friend' the 'phone
To live silently alone

Now I silently grieve
And cannot believe
In my sorrow I find
I am offered no comfort nor guide
Tho' deep in my heart is the 'Almighty'
Filling my heart with 'glee'.

Josephine Foreman

FEAR . . . THE ENEMY

Fear . . .
It lurks here, there, everywhere,
In the past, in the now,
For the future.
How
Do I work through the fear?
Of what?
Of what am I afraid?
The fears of the past
Were real, but past.
Yet they hold me - now.
And I'm afraid
For the future.
But in the past there was no-one
To whom I could take those fears.
I was alone with my silent tears.
As a child, afraid, alone.
Yet she survived to tell the hurt,
To relive the torment, the pain, the fear.
She was no longer alone.
She could come out from behind the drawers. From behind the door
As she felt the love and warmth of someone who cared
And who wanted to listen - and wanted to take away
The fear.
It doesn't belong to today.
It's a remnant from the past,
A legacy I want to leave behind.
But I'm afraid - as I walk on - into the future.

Pip Layne

My Therapy

I find writing poetry
A useful form of therapy.
A good way of allowing me
To express all the things I see.
I must admit I'm not that great,
Can't verbally communicate,
But when I sit down with a pen,
The words flow freely from me then.
Why pay an analyst a fee,
The answer has to come from me.
I've tried that and been criticised.
Psychologists fail to see both sides
And family take a blinkered view.
Mine support me, while yours back you.
So leave me with an empty page,
Counsellors kindly leave the stage.
I've learned to follow my instinct,
A hunch, and truth, are often linked.
I know you lied, but it's too late
Now I am resigned to my fate.
You are believed, and I'm condemned
My poetry's my only friend.
But one day when our children see
It's through your deceit, they abandoned me.
Then you my love, may know my pain,
And if I've gone, these words remain.
Yes I find writing poetry
A useful form of therapy.
A silent voice allowing me
The chance to set my feelings free.

Roger A Carpenter

BRAND NAMES OF THE NINETIES

A black girl who insists that I think
of her in that way labels me 'White Honkie'.
Laughing I tell her to stop giving me
black looks and am snared suddenly
by the term 'racist'.

A white girl proclaims all men idiots 'out
only for one thing and when they get it . . .'
'But what about some women' I protest
and am immediately blocked and charged
with 'sexist'.

At the bus stop I stand with my feet
apart and arms folded across the chest while
promoting comfort then am shifted suddenly to
the shelves a stumbling body language expert
has marked 'authoritarian'.

But I have at least gained *some* recognition
which is better surely than having missed
the brand certificate altogether; unlike
the mass-produced narcissists. And out there
on the pavement how can one unscrew the lid
and sample the contents anyway?

Keith Taylor

Hunting The Hunters

So innocent, trusting
A fragile life
Held in the balance
For sacrifice.

God's beautiful creatures
No chance to defend
Helpless and hopeless
Where does it all end?

And how does it feel
With your trophy held high
Can you sleep, do you weep,
Really understand why?

Who are you, what are you,
Do you really care?
Mankind's sole creator
Looks on in despair.

Karen Jones

Hopes For The Vandal

The sharp crack, the laughter.
  A bend of strength from heavy hands
Of the unbendable, takes much effort.
  But worth it.

The toss of a seat (much loved by those who named)
  Not to care, as they do not count, only us.
Mindless deeds played out at night
  Feeling great, authority missing.

Destruction played out, kicks felt in the mind
  Someone must pay, tough.
Morning light, havoc left, all forgotten.
  Deeds counted, costs mounting.
We pay, why?

Years eat away, more destruction.
  Old men sit, remember youth, regrets?
They do not count, only the young.
  They have paid - we know why.

Joan Ratliffe

LITTER-MONGERS

Dawn breaks, the air is clear today;
Dew on the grass still silver-cold,
Soon shaken from cool flowers away;
Waves slatey-grey; smooth sands pure gold.

It seems so, gazing at the bay.
Light breezes rise, small waves tipped white.
Go, walk the shore at break of day;
This is the time of fairest light . . .

Till trippers come and scatter there
Damp picnic papers down the strand,
And plastic bags and cans, strewn where
Once only seashells starred clean sand.

Why do they come to this far sea,
These coves and beaches miles away,
Who only want to laze and be
Burned by the sun day after day?

It seems they'll never understand,
Though you should tell them, to their shame,
Along this legendary strand
All here was beauty till they came.

But let those come who love the wild
Deep seas, still pools, and echoing caves;
Enchanted by them, like a child
Who runs to meet the great green waves.

Diana Momber

SELF-INFLICTED CURSE

I am treated like a social outcast in my own house,
Because I will not smoke, I'm regarded as worse than a louse.
But I know I would never find pleasure in smelling of smoke,
Waking each morning with dry cough, trying hard not to choke.
I hate the way the wretched fumes infiltrate clothes and hair,
When eating out it is not a condition I want to share.
I'm very strict, and demand that my house is kept smoke-free,
Even though the only one who does not ever smoke is me.
But a smoker's addiction is a self-inflicted curse,
Men standing in the streets bad enough, but women seem worse.
I long for the time of no smoking in all public places,
No chance of fumes wafting into non-smokers' faces.
I am not a health nut on a get-fit-quick fix campaign,
But concerned woman, smell of nicotine makes me complain.

S Mullinger

OUCH!

Lies and gossip,
Of the vicious kind,
A total abhorrence
Of the human mind.
Such behaviour,
In a village is rife,
Causing indefinite pain and strife.

Narrow-minded people,
Not enough to do,
Spending their days,
With a motley crew.
Pleasant to your face,
Until your back is turned,
Stick the knife in and twist it hard.

Telling lies,
To this one and that,
Even criticise
The poor old cat.
Causing misery,
Is their only aim,
Taking pleasure from creating pain.

Send them with sail,
To pastures new,
Across the sea,
To Timbuktu.

Jane Rennie

WITH THE CASH

In the greengrocer's
he really upsets me.
When you go in
he's not always there.
But in the baker's,
which he owns
and which he runs
to make a profit.
There, also along with
the other venture he has.
It's alright for some.
Those with the cast,
but who got him
where he is now?
It's those who shop,
but he never sees that.
My friend Mike says
he feels the same
old muck and you
can never rely on him.
Others all say that
a man from abroad
to run a shop,
he's no good so
who is he but
a money-making upstart
out for a fast buck.
He's a turn-off,
a sorry has-been,
young yet very old.

Richard Clewlow

Litter Bugs

An action seen which makes me bitter
  is the way that some dispose of litter
The authorities have bins on every street
  yet some toss their rubbish at your feet

I think there is something must be done
  as society should be better run
They have a law to fit this crime
  but refuse to use it every time

The foreign tourists to our shore
  say they have never seen the likes before
In their countries it is a bad offence
  so they use their bins which is common sense.

One must be cruel to be kind
  to use the law is right you'll find
For in society if this is neglected
  all those crimes can be expected

Lachlan Taylor

LOOKING BACK

When you feel lonely, and out of sorts
And you think life is passing you by
Just remember the happy times
As you look up to the sky.

Thinking back gives you some sad thoughts
But happy memories too
It's part of the healing process
Some say, this is true.

It's great to say, get on with life
This is easier said than done
Words have a great effect on you
But you have to feel that you've won.

Edith Sweeney

PRIDE IN NOSTALGIA

Age has its compensations, so they say
Who wish to convince themselves, perhaps their friends
That the faint pulse beats of age are not
A whit inferior to the exultations of their youth:
That standing breathless but fulfilled
On some high windy peak is sowing seeds
Of rheumatism in later life
And how much wiser to remain
At valley level, looking up at risk of vertigo.
And all those late night sessions, hearty songs
Delivered with tongue-freeing washings of good ale:
How much more prudent to absorb quite cautiously
Perhaps two halves of palest ale and then creep home
In solemn expectation that tomorrow brings
A bilious headache, retribution for excess.
People who pretend to such sententious crap
Do not deserve a memorable youth.
The only compensation age can give
Is time to think, recall, report
With pride and thankfulness
Those feats we most admired in us
In the rich season. Regret, undoubtedly,
That time has moved them from our grasp
But never, never denigrate, pretend
That we are wiser, better, and well rid
Of what were not but now would be
Excesses. Let our model be
The Wyf of Bath, whose backward look
'Tickleth the hertes rote'.

Bill Johnson

SUPPORTER NO HOOLIGAN

I went over to France on one of the ferries
Saw English hooligans who were merry
They went over to France to watch England play
Most of them ended up being put away.

Fighting broke out, people cut, stabbed or maimed
Lay in hospital never to watch the game
Where is it leading to what's it all fore
Is football becoming an eyesore a bore?

When so-called supporters spoil it for others
Degrade our country our fellow brothers
Then this is the time to stop being aloft
Stand back and weigh up the damage the cost.

Put them in prison don't give them a fine
That's like giving a child one hundred lines
Hard labour wouldn't be too cruel
Then we can get back to the game of football.

S Askew

Why Girls?

Why are girls meant to be fluffy
And play with things that are pink and puffy?
Why must they always cook and clean
And act as if they are programmed machines?
Oh, why must they be quiet and listen
When all they want to do is glisten?

Why can girls not be like boys
Who have lots of dangerous and exciting toys
And who do whatever they want to do
Not worrying about breaking a social taboo?

Oh, why is it that girls have to conform,
To what is considered the female norm?

Sarah Louise Morris

PURPLE DREAMS

Purple dreams and other themes
Are swirling in my head
Women crying, children dying
While we sleep in bed.

Frightened faces, stinking places
See them every day,
Crawling cripples, cause no ripples
It just happens anyway

Sun-baked valleys, shanty alleys
Diseases all around
Soldiers killing, graves are filling
Food cannot be found

Through the ages, written pages
Lessons still not learned
Cannot meddle, backward peddle
Fingers might get burned

Politics make me sick
No money to be made
Just hot air, they don't care
Poverty won't fade

They are human, we are human
This do not forget
Raise your voice, we have the choice
Let us not forget.

Poor or wealthy, sick or healthy
We are full and free
Black or white, this cannot be right
Let's end this misery

What to do, I'm asking you
There must be a way
It bothers me, it's insanity
But peace must come one day

Terry White

Positive Moves

What have we done
to the world.
For we care.

We care
about beautiful places
that're there
disappearing in litter.

Smoky atmosphere
traffic emerging
erratic behaviour
controlling the air.

Appreciate the environment
for we care.

There's solutions
to pollutions
just keep to resolutions.

Don't get disillusioned
or run out of time.
Give it your best.
Get stronger.
'Care'!
Pick up litter,
and don't despair.

Everyone can do it
For we can care.
Stronger and better.
Environment care.

A Isherwood

Appreciation

I risk the cold of soggy feet
To give the birds some food to eat,
Bread and bits of fat and meat.

Clean their little wooden huts
Break the ice on water butts
Fill the holders with peanuts.

Clear a patch of snow from lawn
Grass is looking quite forlorn.
Sprinkle on some golden corn.

On the ice I slip and slide
As I hurry back inside,
Behind the curtain quickly hide.

Seagulls hurry down to feed
Pecking on the corn with speed
Eating each and every seed.

Then a flock of starlings come
Hustling in a raucous scrum
And eating every single crumb.

Then, suddenly away they fly
Into the grey and stormy sky.
Their thanks to me as they fly by
Spatter my windows in a spray
Of spots, saw-edged and dirty grey.

Same procedure every day!

D Griffiths

Designer Woman

Silicone boobs, otherwise size ten,
The perfect Designer Woman for men,
She appears daily on everyone's TV.
The role model, how women should be.

Immaculate make-up conceals all flaws,
Lipstick matching her polished claws,
She works-out religiously in the gym,
With plenty of reserve energy for him.

'Natural', shiny hair is never a mess;
All she attempts is bound for success.
Anyone over size fourteen a disgrace,
Diets glare at us, all over the place.

If we follow them and exercise regimes,
We will be like her, 'normal' it seems,
Which is what our menfolk now expect,
Else, we are found guilty of self-neglect.

Nor are we allowed to mature gracefully;
The menopause is no excuse, with HRT.
Why then, are so many women in my street,
'Overweight', or is it just those I meet?

For eating disorders she must assume blame,
Suggesting all women can, must look the same.
Designer Woman causes her sisters' misery,
Urging us to try and become the perfect She.

We fall into the trap, spending with abandon,
Trying to become like her, a prize to be won.
The Media is controlling us, very skilfully.
Really, we are exactly as God wants us to be.

Janet Hewitt

Bureaucracy And Red Tape

Bureaucracy and red tape
Are things that make me mad
When common sense does not abound
It's really very sad
It's more than my job's worth
Is something often heard
When all that's really needed
Is a sensible word.

Why are they so dogmatic
It causes so much distress
When it could be so different
Not put us under stress.
If only all those bureaucrats
Just really understood
That we who are mere mortals
Do our best to be good.

But you wouldn't really think so
The way they speak to us
It's like being run over
By a double-decker bus.

Constance Chant

Move It

It doesn't take that long - and it isn't that hard,
to succeed they don't need a degree.
They just need to think of others -
instead of incessantly thinking of *me*.

It's second nature to most - done as a matter of course,
but to those who are selfish, please hark -
when you've finished doing your shopping,
put the trolley back in the park.

There's nothing that ruffles my feathers,
or causes my tempter to flare -
than those who load up their shopping
and drive off, leaving trolley 'just there'

Yes, they know someone else will move it,
do they care if it blocks parking lane?
No! they're too busy thinking of only themselves -
and in my book, they're nowt but a pain.

Audrey Woodall

ZANY

There's windmills in the heather
And cows without a moon,
So if we don't have leather
We will all be barefoot soon.

With old soles and litter louts
The muggers and the vandals,
If shoes in price go through the roof
Then just try wearing sandals.

With longer skirts and spit through shirts
There's room for stronger clothes,
With tartan shades and stocking dirks
And rings for through your nose.

If you eat rice that is not nice
Then try a blend of curry,
Your diet then will be in splice
There's somewhere you must hurry.

With old phones and plastic bone
And cats so nice and furry,
There's digital with less of tone
And farms with lots of slurry.

W Robertson

JUST GIVE UP

Why can't you accept that it's too late for penitence?
After all it's been almost two years now.
You say you didn't know what you had
'til I sent you away.
You seem to think I'll believe you
when you tell me you've changed.

A leopard can't change its spots,
And you were the worst kind of animal,
You preyed on my very identity.
Why do you persist in pursuing me?
Your crimes against me were too many,
And too heinous for me to ever forgive, or forget.

I have to see you because of the life we created,
But I don't have any obligation to you,
I have a life of my own and you have to accept
that you have no place in it.
I struggled for so long to break free,
And I will never again be caged.

How could you possibly think
I could feel anything other than revulsion for you?
The slightest touch from you makes my skin crawl.
When you question me I still feel the fear,
And I despise myself for being afraid.

You tried to break me, but you failed,
Now that I am free of you
I intend to stay that way.
You're only wasting your life,
Your breath and your time,
And insulting my intelligence
with your spurious contrition.

Sally Malone

Road Rage

If, by my own hand, purposely,
I spread the road with deadly ammunition,
Broadcast it, like so much evil seed,
I would expect immediate prosecution.

Yet look!
The public highway's strewn with it!
It's shot at bullet speed by passing wheels,
As lethal as the stones from David's sling.
It smashes, gouges, wounds, in all directions,
Leaves every gutter, every pavement,
Littered with spent shells.

Hot tar and chipping stones!
The builders of the ancient Roman roads
Must lie incredulous in their Roman graves.

For me, red mist descends!
Outraged,
I shake a clenched and furious fist
At all the men who sanction
Such a dangerous and a wretched operation.

How dare they!
How dare they spread our roads with ammunition!
Broadcast it, like so much evil seed!
Endanger life and limb and property
With such impunity!

Prosecute them.

Peter W Holt

ROAD RAGE SUBLIMATED

You son of a thousand fathers,
Cutting in on me like that.
Your mother, a cross-eyed camel,
Was born of a diseased cat.

A curse upon your house,
And upon your vehicle, too,
And if you own a horse
May it cast a shoe.

Oh dear me! Just look at that.
Your hubcap's spun off your wheel.
My curse is bearing fruit, I see,
And improving how I feel.

I pray it was an alloy one,
And cost you quite a bit.
I hope you saw the damage done
When I ran over it.

With luck one can't be replaced,
And you must buy another four,
And then, perhaps, at such a cost,
You'll be cutting in no more.

R L Cooper

Miss Right

She's as high as a kite,
that Miss Right,
she'll come down to earth,
and for all that it's worth,
she'll end up dead,
but that's not to be said,
because Miss Right,
considering her height,
always puts up
a very big fight.

Tracey Rush

Bullies

Bullies ought to be stamped on, they're bugs,
Internal thugs.
Getting in the way of simple lives, parasites,
Empty fights.
Squalid thieves enlisting two-faced recruits,
Injected roots.
Displaced humans breaking rank, toxic fiends,
Variable means.
Bullies are to be pitied, made to feel small,
Taught how to crawl.
From crawling to walking held by a lead,
Only then will we succeed.
Bullies walking on the right road, secure,
Demure.

Amanda Louise Thompson

Who Do They Think 'They' Are?

People's superiority and arrogance get up my back.
For the less fortunate feelings and etiquette they lack.
They are the first to moan when postmen, refuse-collectors,
firemen, hospital workers, etc go on strike.
These 'Big Heads' are not as important as they would like!
Who do 'they' think they are!

I find everyone of us belong to a team.
We are all somehow of importance one way or another,
you understand what I mean?
Some have had better opportunities then others in life.
Circumstances, luck, and money play a big role to thrive.
Who do 'they' think they are?

None of us should make the less fortunate look stupid and inferior.
Nobody is perfect and certainly should not think to be superior.
Who do 'they' think they are!
Often forgotten their track?
They do get up my back.
Too many of them are around!

Annemarie Poole

WIND-UPS IN THE WORKPLACE

I see red when the phone rings and,
It's usually someone or some company I've never heard of,
Or we do not do business with,
Wanting a few moments of my time, just to update their data-base;
Sorry no *time*, we're not interested,
And where did you get our name from? Oh! I don't know,
comes the vague response . . .
It's infuriating that any Tom, Dick or Harry can find out any details,
Even down to the shoe size of an employee, with just a key-stroke!
The days of confidentiality are over, *Big Brother* is out there
with a vengeance.
Yuk! to data-base merchants . . .
Whilst trying to total a column of figures, the fax rings,
then the bilge of junk mail,
Commences its final journey, it's normally binned immediately.
But curiosity stops me working just in case the data is relevant;
It never is, just some smut about sex-aids, mobile phones,
credit-help and free holidays;
My waste bin is emptied on daily basis now,
The fax-roll use has increased one hundredfold.
Yuk! to junk mail faxes.
Callers who ask the name of the MD, stating they've spoken to
him/her many times,
How come they don't even know their sex or name then!
Pressure selling after you have stated you're more than happy
With the phone system, accounts system, and we don't wish
to pay for a service,
Which is totally unnecessary thank you.
Callers who ask for the *Proprietor* we are not an hotel or restaurant,
Please get the facts right before ringing . . .
No wonder everyone is so stressed, under pressure and just plain fed up!

Life in an office has simply become a nightmare,
With unwanted faxes, time-wasting phone calls,
and streams of Sales Reps . . .
All pushing their wears, to no avail.
Please leave us alone, let us get on with the job in hand,
Peace is all we ask for, uninterrupted peace . . .
But, it will never happen, because this is the age
of continual *wind-ups* . . .

Amanda-Lea Manning

The Poor Rich

Every day we read them, these tales of stress and strain.
So and so's drugs problem or their 'alcohol abuse'.
Surely they must realise that scant sympathy they'll gain
From spilling all those beans and letting tongues flap far too loose.
I'll admit, it must be awful to have money to buy dope,
From singing, acting, being oneself; no wonder they can't cope!
Come down into the real world where the rest of us still live,
Struggling to make ends meet, yet finding time to give.
Don't whinge and whine of pressures that we just can't understand
Then take an overdose after your rescue's neatly planned.
'A cry for help' would ring more true judged on another scale.
The homeless and the unemployed, the ships that have no sail.
So spare a thought in your 'brave fight' for those with little hope.
No job, no money, nothing left, yet still refuse to mope.
A lesson you may learn from them if you would only see
That everyone has problems:
Folks like you and folks like me.

Joy Sanders